The REGGIE WHITE TOUCH FOOTBALL PLAYBOOK

Winning Plays, Rules, and Safety Tips

Reggie White and Larry Reid

Warrenton Press, Inc.
Warrenton, Virginia

A note to touch football players:
Almost everyone would agree that touch football is safer than tackle football. But that doesn't mean touch football is 100% safe. *No* sport is 100% safe. Over the course of a touch football career, a player is bound to collide with a buddy or two, or lose his or her balance and fall. If you choose to play touch football, you know that the risk of injury exists. It's a part of the game that can never be totally wiped out. Older players who have been inactive for awhile should consider getting a medical checkup before they start playing.

Library of Congress Cataloging in Publication Data

White, Reggie.
    The Reggie White touch football playbook: winning plays, rules, and safety tips/by Reggie White and Larry Reid; illustrations by Millicent Tuman.
    p. cm.
        Includes bibliographical references (p.).
        ISBN 1-880020-00-9 : $9.95
        1.   Touch football–Juvenile literature.
            I. Reid, Larry, 1962-. II. Tuman, Millicent.   III. Title.
    GV952.W48 1991
    796.332'8—dc20   91-25321
                                                                          CIP
                                                                          AC

This book is available at special quantity discounts for bulk purchases for recreational sports classes, sales promotions, premiums, or fund raising. For details write to: Marketing Dept., Warrenton Press, Inc., 31 Pepper Tree Court, Warrenton, VA 22186.

A portion of the proceeds from the sale of this book goes to Hope Palace, located in Maryville, Tennessee. Hope Palace—shown in the photograph above, with Reggie, his wife, Sara, his son, Jeremy, and his daughter, Jecolia—was founded in 1991 by Reggie and Sara to provide quality maternity care for women lacking financial resources. Reggie and Sara wish to expand their program by opening up other Hope Palaces in the near future.

To my wife, Sara, and my other two blessings, Jeremy and Jecolia.

— Reggie

To my wife, Jaci, for believing in me.

— Larry

ACKNOWLEDGEMENTS

The publication of any book is the product of the efforts of many people. The authors wish to acknowledge the help of the following people:

Jim Taft of Pop Warner Football and Fred Mueller of the National Center for Catastrophic Sports Injury Research for reviewing the book and giving their input on safety.

Glenn Schwartzman of SportsPro Management, Inc., and Mike Fink, who got the authors together.

Mitchell Gerber, for his fine editing.

Joe Jones, Jonathan Hodnett, Lance Lerman, Jacquelyn Reid, and Robert Reid, who reviewed draft manuscripts and added their valuable input.

Adam Simons, Deke Shipp, Thomas Howard, Amanda Woody, Brian Gowin, Raven Morgan, Jermaine Porter, Mesle Alemseged, Farid Hotaki, Amro Mohamed, Edward Salgado, Christian Terrazas, Mark Gowin, Kris Southard, and Jackie Waller Russell, who helped make this book more readable for young players.

Ruth & Aaron Reid, Ilene Reid, Samuel Levi Gerber, and Judy Lefkowitz, for their help and support.

Hank Sternberg, Leo Horey, Gregg Harris, Tony Alexis, Steve Arnold, and Ed Carnot, who added their input and support to this project.

Marilyn & Tom Ross, who added their professional and timely consulting help and insight.

USAir, for bending the rules slightly and allowing one of the authors and the photographer to fly to a photo shoot on very short notice.

And of course, Millicent Tuma for all the great illustrations, and Barbara Kinney for the super photographs.

TABLE OF CONTENTS

FOREWORD

At last! A great book written for touch football! *The Reggie White Touch Football Playbook* will give any reader comprehensive knowledge of what touch football is all about. Not only does the book promote winning football, but safety as well.

The easy writing style holds the reader's interest from cover to cover. It's written with the well-conditioned player and also the "weekend warrior" in mind. This book is for everybody! It's a textbook of touch football written in football jargon.

I know that all of you will enjoy this book as much as I did. This is a book for any sports-oriented person's library.

Jim C. Taft,
National Football Commissioner,
Pop Warner Football

INTRODUCTION

You are in the offensive team's huddle in a touch football game. Next touchdown wins. Your teammates look to you for the winning play. Do you know what to call?

Professional football players have playbooks that set out all the offensive and defensive plays their teams can use. College and high school football players have playbooks, too.

But the touch football player has pretty much been forgotten.

Until now!

This playbook sets out the plays and strategies that will help you make the right call in your next touch football game—whether you play with two, three, four, or more players per team. It adds a level of strategy and fun that you just don't get from a quarterback merely telling his receivers "O.K., everybody go out" or "Just get free."

This playbook covers such topics as passing against a man-to-man defense, passing against a zone, calling audibles at the line of scrimmage, playing a zone defense, and calling a blitz.

Section 1 provides rule guidelines for players who aren't familiar with touch football. Section 2 discusses the fundamental skills that all football players should master to make the game more fun. Section 3 covers offense. Section 4 covers defense. Section 5 contains safety tips, so you can play safe—as well as smart—touch football. Section 6, which is helpful for beginners, contains a glossary of football terms and a list of recommended football books.

Now you're ready to start reading this playbook and using it to play winning touch football. But don't use just these plays. With this playbook as a guide, make up your own. Then test them out and see how they work.

Soon, after reading this playbook, you'll find yourself in that huddle at the end of the game. And when your teammates look to you to call the winning play, you'll be ready!

RULE GUIDELINES

There are different ways to play touch football. You can use the rules in this section or make up your own to fit your situation.

To get started, all you need is a football, some open space to set up a field, and some players.

The Field

On the next page is an illustration showing the difference between a professional football field and a touch football field. A professional football field is 120 yards long and 53⅓ yards wide. A touch football field is about half as big.

Both the professional football field and the touch football field have **goal lines** and **end zones**. This is where touchdowns are scored. And each has **sidelines** and **end lines**—with any area outside the sidelines and end lines being **out of bounds**.

The line going across the middle of each field is known as **midfield**.

The Professional Football Field

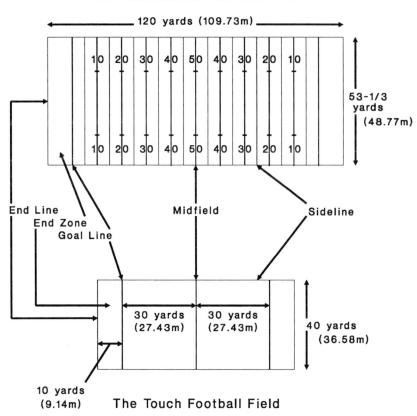

Comparison between a professional football field and an average touch football field.

The Players

To play a touch football game, you will need at least three players:

1. A **quarterback** (the player who throws the football).
2. A **receiver** (the player who catches the football).
3. A **defender** (the player who tries to stop the receiver from catching the football).

Usually a game is played with more players. Three to seven players per team is best.

If you have an odd number of players, you can make one player the quarterback for both teams.

The quarterback delivers the pass in this seven-player touch football game.

The Offense

The objective is to score more **touchdowns** than the other team. In a professional game, a touchdown is worth six points, with the point-after kick counting for an additional point. You can forget about the kick and just make each touchdown worth seven points.

To score a touchdown, the team on **offense**—the team with the football—tries to get one of its players into the other team's end zone with the ball. As illustrated below, this can be done in three different ways:

1. A receiver in the end zone catches a pass.

2. A receiver catches a pass and runs into the end zone.

3. A player simply runs into the end zone with the ball.

The defender (light shirt) jumps in front of the receiver for the interception.

The Defense

The team on defense—the team without the football—tries to stop the other team from scoring a touchdown. They do this by tagging the player who has the ball, or by trying to catch or knock down a pass. If a defender catches a pass, known as making an **interception**, the defender can run with the ball towards the other team's end zone and try to score a touchdown.

In touch football, the defenders stop the offense by tagging (rather than tackling) the player with the ball. A play is over when the ball carrier is tagged.

To tag the ball carrier in a two-hand touch football game, a defender has to touch the ball carrier with both hands *at the same time*. In a one-hand touch game, a defender can tag the ball carrier with only one hand. It's up to you which way to play.

The defender tags the ball carrier with both hands to stop the play.

A defensive team scores a "safety" when one of the defenders tags the ball carrier behind the ball carrier's own goal line. The defense is awarded two points for a safety.

To make matters worse for the offensive team whose player was caught behind the goal line, they also have to kick-off to the other team.

Starting a Game

To start a game, you can toss a coin to see which team gets the football first. Then a player from the other team **kicks-off**, as illustrated below. Kick-offs are also made by a team after scoring a touchdown.

A kick-off

A kick-off should be made from about halfway between the kicking team's goal line and midfield. A player from the receiving team catches the kick-off and follows his or her blockers up the field until being tagged.

Returning a kick-off

Playing Offense

The offensive team starts from where the kick returner was tagged. The imaginary line running across the field at that spot is the **line of scrimmage**.

A play starts at the line of scrimmage with the quarterback calling **signals**. Signals can be nothing more than the words "Ready-Set-Hike," or they can be coded plays that the quarterback shouts to the receivers (Chapter 9).

No player from either team is allowed to cross the line of scrimmage until the quarterback "snaps" the ball by yelling "Hike." A penalty—known as **"off-sides"**—occurs when a player from either team crosses the line of scrimmage before the ball is snapped.

> *When a penalty is committed, the team that didn't commit the penalty can:*
>   1. *Accept the penalty, and the last play is replayed.*
>   2. *Decline the penalty, and the game goes on as if the penalty never happened.*

When the quarterback yells "Hike," the receivers start running their pass patterns, and the **rusher**—the defensive player covering the quarterback—starts counting out loud to four or five. Meanwhile, the quarterback either passes the football to one of the receivers, laterals the ball to another player for a run, or runs with the ball himself.

If the quarterback throws the football and it's not caught—an **incomplete pass**—the play is over. If the receiver catches the football, the play is over when the receiver is tagged or goes out of bounds. A play is also over if the rusher finishes counting and tags the quarterback behind the line of scrimmage for a loss of yardage while the quarterback is still holding the ball—called a **sack**.

After a completed pass, a run, or a sack, the new line of scrimmage is where the ball carrier was tagged. After an incomplete pass, the line of scrimmage stays the same.

Making a First Down

If you are playing on a small field, the offense should get four plays, or **"downs,"** to score a touchdown. If they don't score, the football goes over to the other team, and then they have four downs. They go in the opposite direction, starting from the old line of scrimmage.

Reggie gets ready to rush a nervous quarterback, who is sure glad to be playing touch, rather than tackle, football.

Passes and Laterals

*A football thrown forward to a teammate is called a **pass**. You are allowed to throw only one pass per play.*

*A football thrown sideways or backwards is called a **lateral**. There is no limit to the number of laterals you can throw.*

A pass is illegal if it is thrown:

1. *From in front of the line of scrimmage.*
2. *After a pass has already been thrown in the same play.*
3. *During a kick-off or punt return.*

If an illegal pass is thrown, the play is automatically over, and the new line of scrimmage is at the spot where the illegal pass was thrown from.

*Safety Tip: Use a rule that the play is automatically over if the ball carrier drops the football—known as a **fumble**—or if the ball carrier falls to the ground. This prevents injuries that can be caused by players smashing into each other chasing after a loose ball or by players diving on a ball carrier who is on the ground. The new line of scrimmage is where the ball was dropped or the ball carrier fell.*

After the receiver catches the pass, the new line of scrimmage will be at the point where the receiver is tagged.

If you are playing on a bigger field, where it would be very hard to score a touchdown in just four downs, you may want to allow the offense to make a **"first down."** If it does, it then gets another four downs to score a touchdown.

A first down can be earned in different ways, depending on which best fits your situation. One way is by reaching midfield. Another way is by gaining a certain amount of yardage—maybe ten yards, like in the pros. Another way is by completing at least three passes in four downs.

Punting

If you are on offense and it is fourth down, you need to decide whether to go for the touchdown or first down, or to **punt**. A punt is illustrated on the next page.

If you try to make the touchdown or first down and are not successful, the ball goes over to the other team at your line of scrimmage. If it's close to your own end zone, you will probably want to punt.

The team receiving the punt treats it just like a kick-off. The player who catches the punt runs up the field behind blockers.

Safety Tip: Use a rule that the offense has to tell the defense if it will punt. If the offense chooses to punt, the defensive team drops back and fields the punt like a kick-off. This prevents injuries that can be caused by a defensive player rushing into the punter while the punter is kicking the ball.

Blocking

On running plays and kick and punt returns, if you are not the ball carrier, you will want to block. "Blocking" means getting in the way of a defender with your chest and shoulders to prevent the defender from tagging the ball carrier. Good blocking form is shown in the photograph on the next page.

Blocking a defender in the back is a penalty, known as "clipping." See page 29.

A punt

The blocker (dark shirt) keeps his feet wide apart for good balance and positions his body between the ball carrier and the defender.

The End of the Game

Before starting a touch football game, the two teams should agree on how many points it will take to win. Of course, if you prefer, you can just keep playing until you have to go home.

Clipping

FUNDAMENTALS

1 *Throwing the Football: The Quarterback*

To be a good quarterback, you must master throwing the football. The best play in the world won't work if you can't get the ball to your receiver.

To learn how to throw a football, pick one up and start practicing.

Grip the ball as in the illustration on page 32. You should hold the ball towards the back. At least two of your fingers should grab the laces, and your thumb should wrap around the bottom of the ball.

Don't press the palm of your hand against the football. Fingertip control—not an overly tight grip—is the key to throwing a tight spiral instead of a wobbly pass. If your hand is too small to firmly grip a professional-size football, then learn to throw by using a mini-size football.

Hold the football with both hands—as illustrated on the next page. Keep it level with your chin, and keep it steady. Your weight should be on the balls of your feet, with your feet comfortably spaced apart. If you are right-handed, your left foot should be forward (if you are left-handed, you should reverse these directions all the way through).

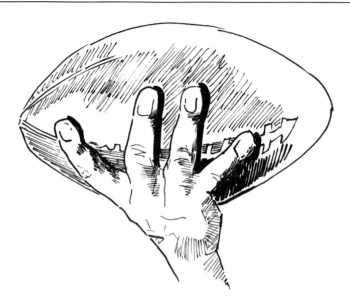

Gripping the football

Your body should be turned sideways so that your left side is facing your target. To see the target, you will need to turn your head to the left. Now, you're ready to throw.

Bring the football back to your ear and then step toward your target with your left foot and fire away, keeping your elbow pointed straight at the target until you throw. If you step towards your target, your weight will naturally shift from your back foot (the right foot if you are right-handed) to your front foot as your arm comes forward.

Make sure that you follow through with your arm for distance and accuracy. And let your back foot come forward from the momentum of your weight shift.

The key to throwing well is practice. The more you practice, the better you will get. The best way to practice is to throw the football to a receiver who is running the pass patterns set out in Chapter 4.

Throwing the football

Always try to "lead the receiver." In other words, don't throw the football to where the receiver is—throw the football to where the receiver *is going to be*. When the receiver can catch your passes in full stride, without slowing down, you know you have become a good passer.

But there is a lot more to playing quarterback than knowing how to throw the football. The quarterback is the most important offensive player on the field and is usually responsible for calling the plays. The quarterback can't just jump on the field and start firing away. He or she must know the plays, and where all the offensive players should be during each play.

Great quarterbacks like Phil Simms, Joe Montana, and my teammate, Randall Cunningham, have excellent "field vision." Field vision is more than just having good eyesight. It's the ability to see the entire field at once and to know where a receiver will come free.

The most important test of field vision is your ability to see *all* of your receivers. Sure, you need to be able to find the receiver you want to throw to—known as the **primary receiver**. But you also need to be able to find your **secondary receivers**—the ones you look to if the primary receiver is covered.

Great quarterbacks have the ability to see the whole field at once.

"Hey, this isn't so easy."

If you were inside the brain of a really great quarterback like Phil Simms dropping back to throw a pass during a game, it might sound a little like this:

"OK, look to the left to fool the defense. Now look for Stephen going straight up the right side. Covered. OK, what about Mark coming across the middle? Covered. OK, what about Dave staying short on the right side? Bingo!"

The amazing thing about all this thinking and looking is that it all happens in about *four seconds*. Hard to believe, isn't it?

The only way for you to improve your field vision so that you can find the open receiver is to study and know each of your plays. That way, you will be able to see each play unfold in your head long before the play actually unfolds on the field.

This extra level of preparation may seem like a lot of hard work. But it could mean the difference between being a good quarterback and being a great one.

Here are some other tips to help you become a great Quarterback:

1. Don't give away where you will be throwing the football by staring in that direction. Good defenders will be "reading your eyes" to guess where the ball is going. Look in the opposite direction until right before throwing the ball.

2. In the huddle, don't look or point at the receivers when calling the pass patterns. Often, the other team will be watching you to see who will be getting the ball.

3. Adjust for weather conditions such as wind and rain. Receivers run more slowly and turn less sharply when the field is slick.

4. Release the football quickly. Practice throwing the ball *before* the receiver is actually open. If you wait to throw the ball until the receiver is open, the receiver could be covered by the time the pass gets there.

To avoid getting sacked, sometimes a quarterback has to throw a pass before knowing if the receiver will be open.

5. Take a little of the zip off your passes when you are throwing for short yardage. A good pass is one the receiver can catch—not one that looks good because it was thrown hard.

6. Ask your teammates for their ideas for plays. Sometimes they see weaknesses in the defense that you don't.

2 Catching the Football: The Receivers

Quarterbacks like to throw to open receivers. If the receiver is open, there will be a better chance of the pass being completed. Quarterbacks also like to throw to "sure-handed receivers"—those who can be counted on to make the catch. Quarterbacks hate throwing to receivers who always seem to be covered tightly by their defenders, or who drop passes that should have been caught.

The lesson to be learned here is simple. The better you are at getting free and holding on to the football, the more passes will come your way.

The good news for you is that good receivers are made, not born. You can turn yourself into a good receiver, one the quarterback depends on and throws to often, by learning the fundamental skills of pass catching and by practicing your pass patterns.

The three keys to being a good receiver are running sharp pass patterns, concentrating on the football, and having "soft hands."

It might surprise you that speed isn't one of the key ingredients to being a good receiver. But the truth is, some of the best receivers in the National Football League have not been speedsters.

Of course, speed helps. It's great to be able to outrun your defender. But if all you have is speed, a smart defender will

quickly learn to back off from the line of scrimmage a couple
of extra steps to take away your advantage.

Look out Jerry Rice!

Running Sharp Pass Patterns

The difference between running a sharp pass pattern and
running a sloppy one is illustrated on the following page.

Notice how the defender is forced to cover more ground
when the receiver runs the sharper pattern. Although this extra
distance may seem small, it could be the difference between
your being open to catch the pass or not.

Remember, the quarterback will be deciding whether or not
to throw the football to you depending on the number of steps
between you and the defender. Each step that you can put
between yourself and the defender will make it more likely
that the quarterback will throw you the ball.

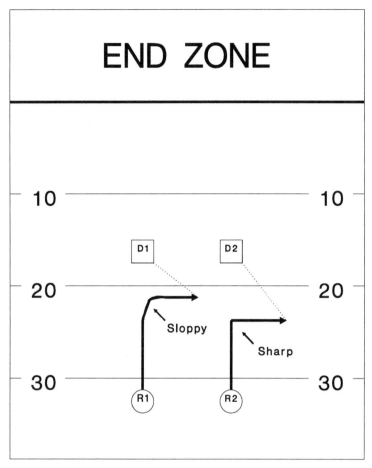

Receiver R1 runs a sloppy pass pattern while Receiver R2 runs a sharp pass pattern. Notice how much further Defender D2 has to go to get to Receiver R2 than Defender D1 has to go to get to Receiver R1.

Concentrating on the Football

Great receivers are able to focus all their attention on the football when it's in the air. All they see is the football. All they are thinking of doing is catching the ball.

Focus all your concentration on the ball.

Receivers who can't focus their concentration on the football end up dropping a lot of passes they should have caught. When a professional receiver drops a pass, often the television announcer says, "the receiver heard footsteps." What the announcer means is that the receiver was so worried about being hit by a defender that he stopped concentrating on the pass.

When the football is in the air, you can't afford to be worrying about what the defenders are doing. Or worrying about passes you might have dropped before—that's in the past. Or worrying about what you are going to do with the football after you've caught it—that's in the future.

All of your concentration must be on the football that you are about to catch. It's the only thing that counts.

Having "Soft Hands"

Good receivers keep their arms and hands relaxed and away from their bodies when catching a pass. They know that passes have a nasty habit of bouncing off chests and stiff fingers.

When you are preparing to catch a football, you should extend your arms and stretch out your fingers, but not stiffly. Then follow the ball with your eyes all the way into your hands. NEVER TAKE YOUR EYES OFF THE BALL!

When the ball hits your hands there needs to be some give in them so the ball comes to rest softly. As soon as possible, bring the football into your body and tuck it away.

Here are some other tips to help you become a good receiver.

1. When making a sharp turn—or "cut"—to the left, push hard off your right foot. When cutting right, push off your left foot.

2. When you can, come back toward the quarterback to catch the football. This will make it harder for the defender to get in front of you to break up the pass.

3. Don't ever give up on a pass pattern and stop running. Even if you are covered, the quarterback might throw the football anyway. If you stop running, you could be giving the defense an easy interception. If a play breaks down, run to an open spot of the field and wave your arms to get the quarterback's attention.

4. Don't be lazy. Run all your pass patterns with the same effort—even if you aren't the primary receiver. This will force your defender to cover you and keep him or her from breaking up a pass to another receiver.

5. Don't give away where you will be running your pass pattern by looking that way when you line up at the line of scrimmage.

6. Some defenders will try to scare you into dropping a pass by yelling when you are about to make a catch. Don't let them beat you with this trick. Tune the defender out. Remember, it's only noise. Concentrate on making the catch.

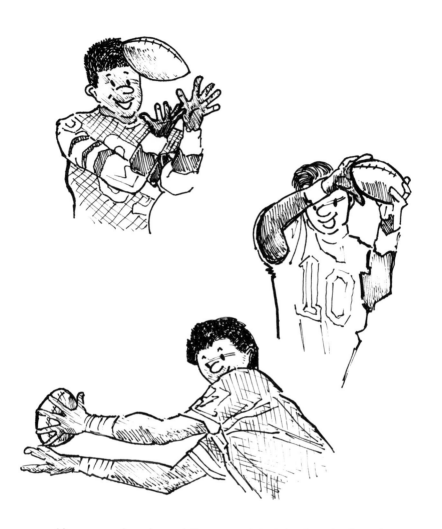

Keep your hands and fingers outstretched and relaxed.

3 *Stopping the Play: The Defenders*

In a touch football game, there are two different types of defensive positions: rusher and pass defender.

The rusher stands at the line of scrimmage across from the quarterback. After counting out loud to four or five, the rusher races across the line of scrimmage and tries to tag the quarterback.

To be a good rusher, you need to be able to tag the quarterback without letting the quarterback get by you for a long run. The key to doing this is to never leave your feet unless you're sure the quarterback will actually throw the ball. If you jump to block a pass and the quarterback doesn't throw the ball, you'll be flying helplessly in the air while the quarterback runs around you and up the field.

Most of the time that you play defense, you will be in **man-to-man** coverage. In man-to-man coverage, the rusher covers the quarterback, and each of the other defenders covers one receiver.

Playing defense against a speedy receiver can be a little scary. But it can also be exciting if you are able to shut the receiver down without a touchdown. To play tough defense against a good receiver, you will need to master the fundamental defensive skills.

47

Don't leave your feet unless you're sure the quarterback is throwing the ball.

Line up across the line of scrimmage from the receiver. Face him or her and keep your feet comfortably spaced apart. You should be five to ten yards from the line of scrimmage. Remember to always give a speedy receiver a little extra room.

Start backpedaling as soon as the receiver starts running towards you. When the receiver cuts to the right or left, so do you. Stop backpedaling and try to run alongside the receiver.

Never keep backpedaling if the receiver is running at full speed up the field. If you do, the receiver will blow right by you.

The defender should backpedal as the receiver comes toward him.

And never turn your back on a receiver—even if the receiver changes direction after making his first cut. If the receiver changes direction, you should pivot so that you can see the receiver at all times, like the defender in the illustration below.

Always pivot instead of turning your back on a receiver.

The only time you should take your eyes off the receiver is when you see the receiver looking back for the pass. This lets you know that you should be looking for the pass, too. Try to knock it down or intercept it if you can.

A common penalty called against pass defenders is known as **"pass interference."** It's illustrated below. Pass interference occurs when a defender makes contact with a receiver who is trying to catch a pass. If the contact is only very slight, however, a penalty should not be called.

Pass interference

Keep in mind that a defender is allowed to bump or block a receiver *at the line of scrimmage* without a penalty being called. This is known as the **bump-and-run**.

To use the bump-and-run, line up across from the receiver about one yard from the line of scrimmage. When the quarterback snaps the ball, bump the receiver away from the quarterback, as in the photograph below. Then, run alongside the receiver up the field.

By forcing the receiver to the outside of the field, you will make the quarterback throw a longer pass and give yourself a better angle for an interception. And bumping the receiver should slow him down. It may even prevent the receiver from running his or her pattern altogether.

The defender (on the right) bumps the receiver at the line of scrimmage.

Here are some other tips to help you play tough defense.

1. To see which way a ball carrier or a receiver is really going, watch his *waist*. Because the waist is a person's

center of gravity, whichever way it's going is the way the rest of him is going.

Watch the ball carrier's waist to see which way he is going.

2. On a short pass, don't come forward towards the line of scrimmage until the football is in the air. Otherwise, the receiver can fake the short pass and race by you when you come forward.

3. All football players have favorite plays that they use in certain situations. Heads-up defenders know this and try to guess what play an offensive team will call. If you can guess correctly, you may be able to pick up an easy interception by beating the receiver to the football.

4. The most important tip to playing good man-to-man
   defense is to NEVER LET YOUR RECEIVER GET
   BEHIND YOU!

It's simple. The more passes the offense has to throw to
score a touchdown, the better the chances that you'll make an
interception, or that the quarterback will throw a couple of
incomplete passes. In other words, make the offense beat you
with three or four short passes—not one long pass.

Of course, there will be times when you'll want to gamble
and try to knock down or even intercept a short pass—on third
or fourth down and short yardage, for example. That's fine.
Just let your teammates know when you're going to gamble.
That way, at least they'll be ready to run after your receiver
in case you get burned.

Another tip to playing tough defense is to look mean.

OFFENSIVE PLAYS

4 *The Basic Pass Patterns*

Before you can start calling plays that burn your buddies for touchdowns, you need to learn the basic pass patterns. That's because plays are made up of receivers running different pass patterns.

When you read the diagrams on the following pages, don't worry if you have more or fewer players than those shown in the diagrams. All you have to do is add or subtract pass patterns, depending on your situation. Just make sure that if you add patterns, your receivers won't be running into each other.

The following key should help you understand the symbols contained in the diagrams.

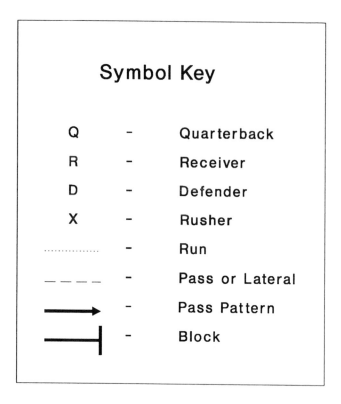

The basic football pass patterns are:
  (1) the **slant-in**,
  (2) the **slant-out**,
  (3) the **down-and-in** (also known as a "square-in,"
     or "in" for short),
  (4) the **down-and-out** (also known as a "square-out," or "out" for short),
  (5) the **hook-in**,
  (6) the **hook-out**,
  (7) the **post**,
  (8) the **flag** (also known as a "corner"), and
  (9) the **fly** (also known as an "up").

These patterns are set out in the diagrams on the following pages.

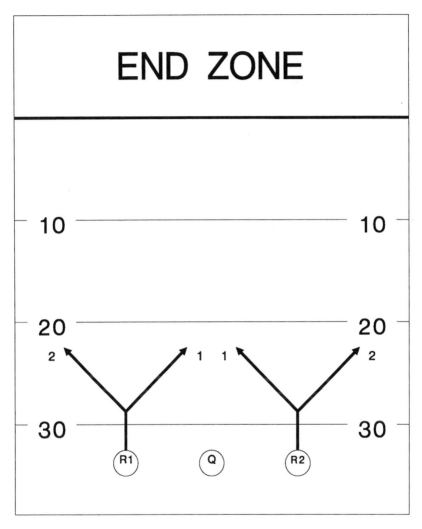

Diagram 1: The (1) Slant-in and (2) Slant-out

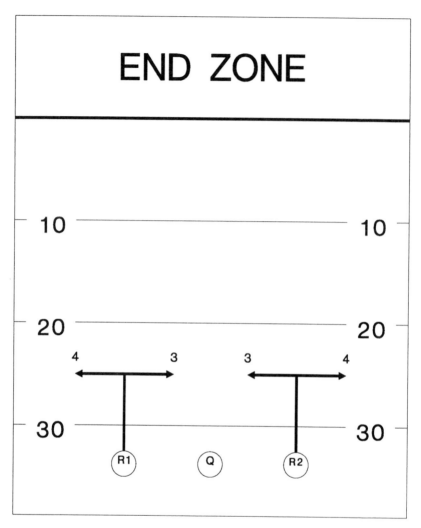

Diagram 2: The (3) Down-and-In and (4) Down-and-Out

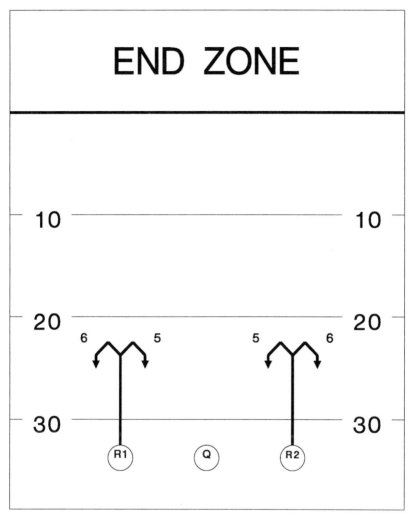

Diagram 3: The (5) Hook-in and (6) Hook-out.

61

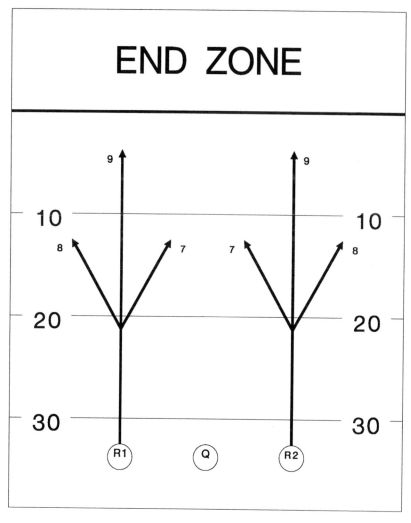

Diagram 4: The (7) Post, (8) Flag, and (9) Fly

The basic pass patterns can be combined in many different ways. Some good combinations are set out in Diagrams 5 and 6.

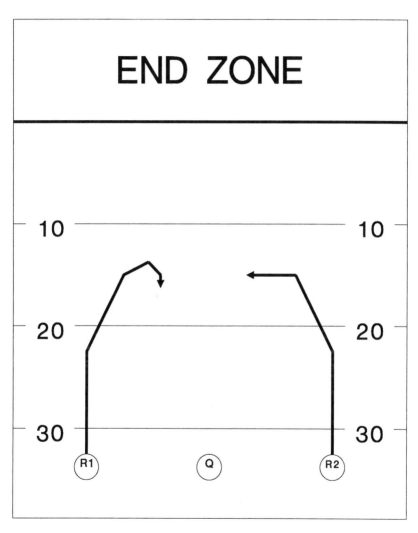

Diagram 5: R1 runs a Post-Hook; R2 runs a Post-In.

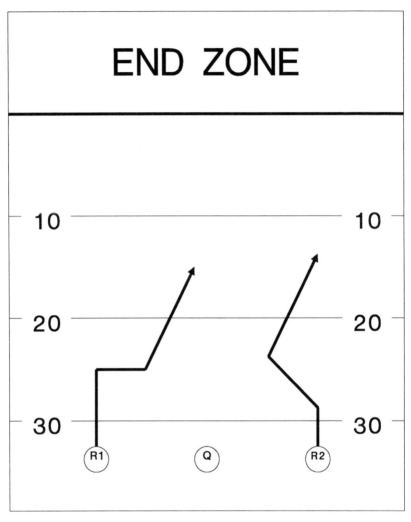

Diagram 6: R1 runs an In-Post; R2 runs a Slant-in-Flag.

5 Passing Against a Man-to-Man Defense

A defense is in man-to-man coverage when each defender covers one specific offensive player. The rusher guards the quarterback while the other defenders cover the receivers.

Any of the pass patterns diagrammed in the previous chapter can be used against man-to-man coverage. But all of those patterns will work better—and free up receivers more often—if they are used together, in a planned attack.

For example, if you want to gain five to seven yards by sending R4 on a down-and-in pattern, but defender D4 has been covering R4 like a blanket, try using the **down-and-in criss-cross.** It's shown in Diagram 7 on the next page.

As you can see, R3 runs a flag pattern just to the inside of D4. In this way, D4 is forced to run around both R3 and D3. This is known as "screening the defender." It gives R4 the one or two steps he needs to come free and catch the down-and-in pass over the middle.

One word of caution about screening the defender: The receiver who sets the screen (R3 in Diagram 7) must not actually make contact with the defender, or a penalty—known as **"picking the defender"**—will be called. Merely running closely by the defender is a legal screen—actually hitting the defender is an illegal pick.

Notice in Diagram 7 that if R4, the primary receiver, isn't open, Q can throw the football to R1 or R2, the secondary receivers. As in the diagram, call patterns for your secondary receivers that will make it easy for you to find them if the primary receiver is covered.

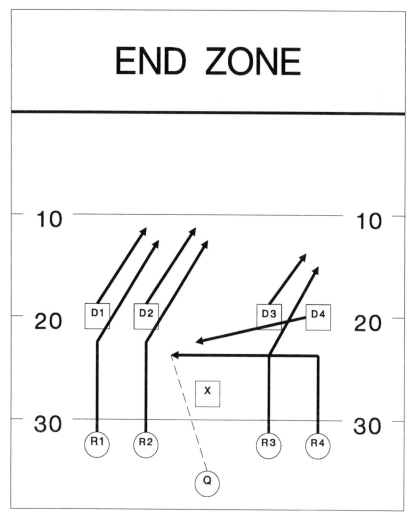

Diagram 7: R3 and R4 run a Down-and-In Criss-Cross.

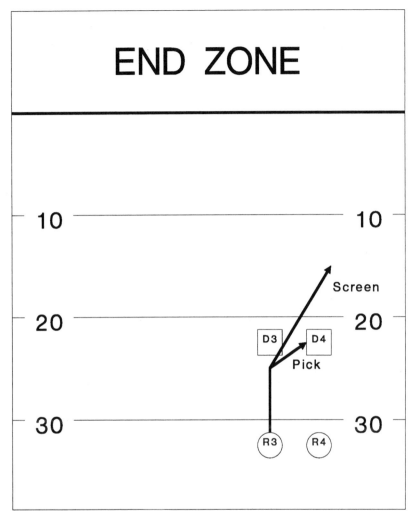

Diagram 8: Legal Screen vs. Illegal Pick.

Also notice what might have happened if R4 had gotten a step or two on D4, caught the ball, and then started running up the field. Who's going to stop R4?

As you can see from the diagram, unless D4 can catch R4 from behind, it's off to the races. That's because D4 will have no help from D1 or D2, who followed their receivers across the field.

Now you can see the three necessary ingredients to any good passing play:

1. A primary receiver;

2. One or two secondary receivers; and

3. Room to run for the primary receiver after the catch is made.

A good version of the down-and-in criss-cross is the **double screen down-and-in criss-cross**. In this play, as set out in Diagram 9 on the next page, both R2 and R3 run to the inside of D4, providing a **double screen** for R4. For D4 to cover R4 cutting across the middle, D4 will have to get around R2 and R3 as well as D2 and D3. With all this traffic in D4's way, there is a good chance that primary receiver R4 will be wide open over the middle.

To clear the left side of the field so R4 will have some running room after catching the ball, you could send R1 on a post pattern to the right side of the field. R1 can be your secondary receiver.

The opposite of the down-and-in criss-cross is the **down-and-out criss-cross**. As you can see in Diagram 10 on page 70, R4 runs by D3 to the outside and screens D3 away from primary receiver R3, who cuts to the outside. You can use R1 on a down-and-in as your secondary receiver.

The best time to use the down-and-in criss-cross or the down-and-out criss-cross is when you need only five to ten yards. These plays should also be used when you want to draw the defenders in closer to the line of scrimmage to set up the use of longer passes later on.

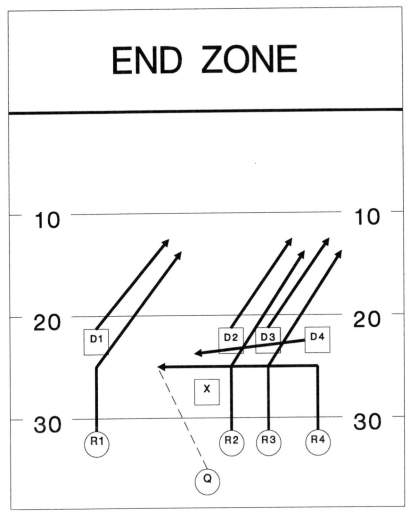

Diagram 9: The Double Screen Down-and-In Criss-Cross.

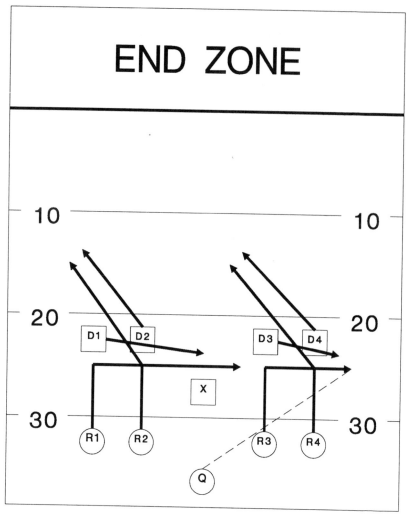

Diagram 10: The Down-and-Out Criss-Cross.

A good play to use when a defender has been covering one of the receivers very tightly from the line of scrimmage is the **down, out, and up,** run by R4 in Diagram 11 on the next page.

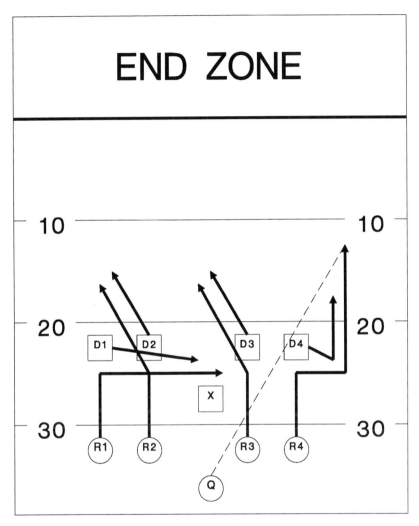

Diagram 11: R4 burns D4 on a Down-Out-and-Up pattern.

Both the receiver and the quarterback will want to fake the defender into believing that they are going for the short yardage down-and-out. The receiver fakes the defender by looking back for the pass at the end of the down-and-out portion of the pattern. At the same time, the quarterback does his or her part by pretending to throw the football (known as a "pump fake") for the down-and-out.

Great times to run this play are when you have a play to waste—on first down, or even second down if you have only short yardage to go. A riskier time to use this play is on third or fourth down when you need only short yardage. But maybe that's when the defense will least expect it.

A good play to call after using a couple of criss-cross patterns is the **fake criss-cross**, shown in Diagram 12 on the next page. R3 and R4 come together as if they are going to cross, and then they each break back the other way, with R3 running a slant-in and R4 running a slant-out.

In Diagram 13 on page 74 are three good one-on-one pass patterns against man-to-man coverage: the **lightning bolt**, the **post-flag**, and the **fly**. These patterns should be used when you think one of your receivers can beat his or her defender without the help of a screen.

To help free up a receiver who has been getting bumped at the line of scrimmage, you can send the receiver **in motion** before the play starts. Because it's always harder to hit a moving target, sending the receiver in motion should make it easier for the receiver to get by the defender and up the field.

To send a receiver in motion, the quarterback must call a signal such as "Set" to start the receiver moving parallel to the line of scrimmage. Until the ball is snapped, the receiver isn't allowed to move forward. Then, when the quarterback calls "Hike," the receiver turns up the field and runs his pattern.

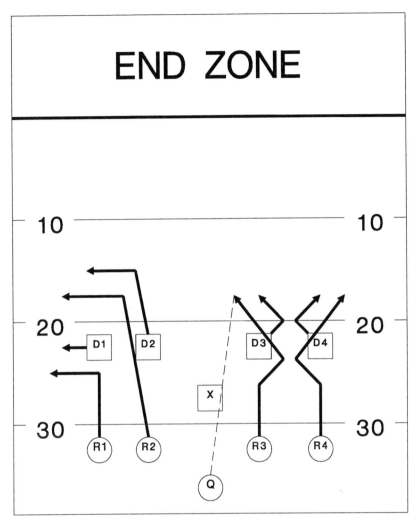

Diagram 12: R3 and R4 run a Fake Criss-Cross.

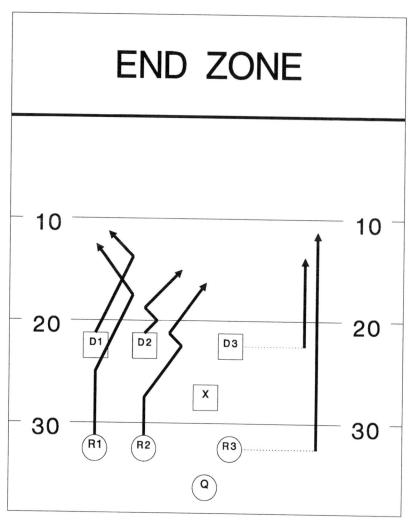

Diagram 13: R1 runs a Post-Flag; R2 runs a Lightning Bolt; and R3 runs a Fly after starting in motion.

6 *Passing Against a Zone Defense*

Sometimes the defensive team will try to confuse you by changing from man-to-man coverage into **zone** coverage. When a defense is in zone coverage, the rusher covers the quarterback and each of the other defenders covers a specific portion, or zone, of the field instead of a specific receiver.

Passing against a zone defense is very different from passing against a man-to-man defense. The biggest difference is that the same criss-cross patterns that work so well against man-to-man coverage won't work nearly as well against a zone.

That's because the defenders won't be trying to stay close to specific receivers. They'll be happy to just sit back in their zones and wait for the quarterback to throw the ball.

The key to passing against a zone defense is to overload or "flood" one defender's zone and, in effect, make the defender cover more than one receiver. When this happens, one of the receivers will have found a "seam" in the zone and be open.

An example of this is shown in Diagram 14 on the next page. In the diagram, the defenders are playing what's called a **2-2 zone**, with two defenders close to the line of scrimmage, two defenders deep, and the rusher covering the quarterback. The first number refers to the number of pass defenders playing close to the line of scrimmage, while the second number refers to the deeper pass defenders. In the diagram, the circular area around each defender is the zone for which the defender is responsible.

When faced with a zone defense, the quarterback should look to overload one side of the field. In the diagram, Q overloads the right side. R3 runs a flag pattern to the outside of the field, and R4 runs a down-and-out.

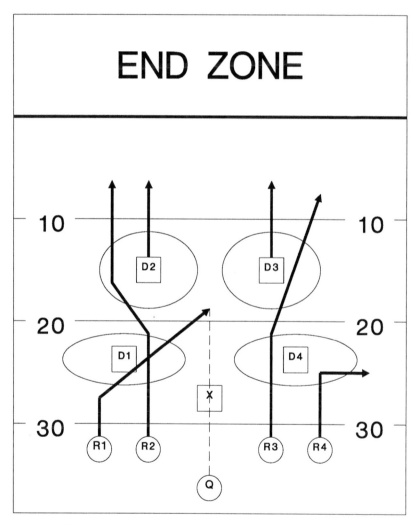

Diagram 14: R1 finds a seam in the 2-2 Zone.

The key to making this play work is the pattern of R2. R2 needs to run to the inside of D1 and then to the outside of D2 and try to fake both defenders into believing that the pass is coming that way. Q should help by using a pump fake in that direction. Meanwhile, R1 should be cutting to the middle of the field, which should be wide open.

Although the previous diagram dealt with a 2-2 zone, you will find that a zone defense works better—and defenders will use a zone more often—when there are more than five players on each team. This is because each defender will be responsible for a smaller portion of the field.

On the next two pages are plays you can use against a **3-2 zone** (three pass defenders up close, two pass defenders deep) and a **2-3 zone**, two forms of zone defense that require six players. If you are playing in an even bigger game, and are up against a **3-3 zone** or a **4-3 zone**, for example, just remember to use these plays as guides and draw up your own plays to flood a defender's zone. If you end up with more receivers than defenders in an area, one of the receivers will be free.

As you can see from the Diagram 16, a hook pattern is very good against a zone. The receiver will want to find a seam in the zone, hook back to the quarterback, and then wait for the pass.

Another good pass pattern to use against a zone defense is the post-flag, shown earlier in Diagram 13. Because the receiver who runs a post-flag will be running to the outside of the field, one of the major benefits of the zone defense—the ability of the defenders to help each other—will be taken away.

Often, a defense will use a zone on third or fourth down if the offense needs long yardage. A play that can be used in this situation is the **deep overload**.

In this play, as shown in Diagram 17, R4 runs a long post while R5 runs a deep down-and-out. R2 then overloads the zone by running a post between R4 and R5. The primary receiver is R2, but look for R5 first because often R5 will be open immediately upon his or her break to the outside. And looking at R5 will draw D5 to R5, opening up the deep right corner of the field for R2.

Against a 3-2 zone, try using a play like this one.

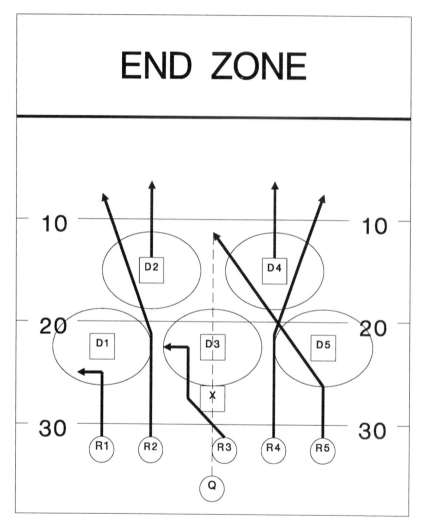

Diagram 15: R2 and R4 take the two deep defenders long while R5 finds the deep middle of the field wide open.

Against a 2-3 zone, try using a play like this one.

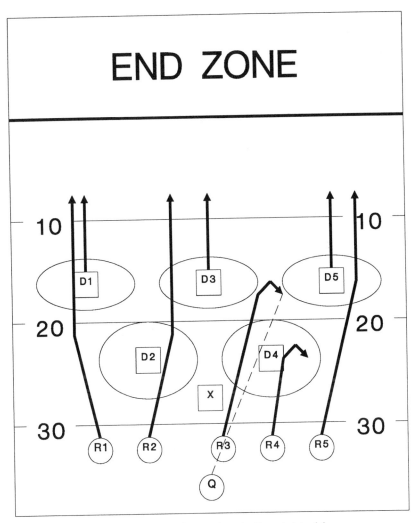

Diagram 16: Q overloads the right side, opening up a seam for R3.

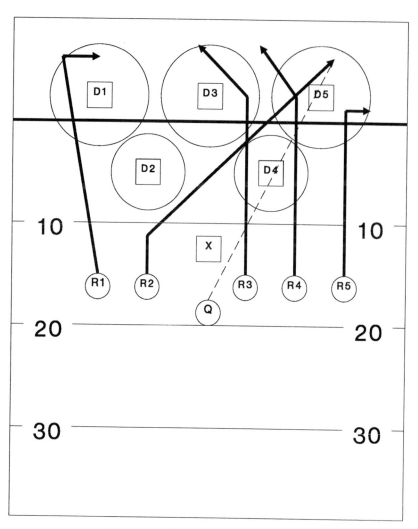

Diagram 17: The Deep Overload

Sometimes, a defense will use a **goal line zone** when the offense is very close to scoring a touchdown. In this defense, as shown in Diagram 18 on the next page, the defenders form a straight line across the goal line instead of having some defenders line up close to the line of scrimmage and others deep.

To beat the goal line zone, send a couple of receivers just over the goal line to one side of the field and have another receiver trail across the back of the end zone to that same side. The quarterback should fake a pass to one of the receivers just over the goal line, to force the defenders to come up to the front of the end zone. Then the quarterback can throw the ball over their heads to the trailing receiver in the back of the end zone.

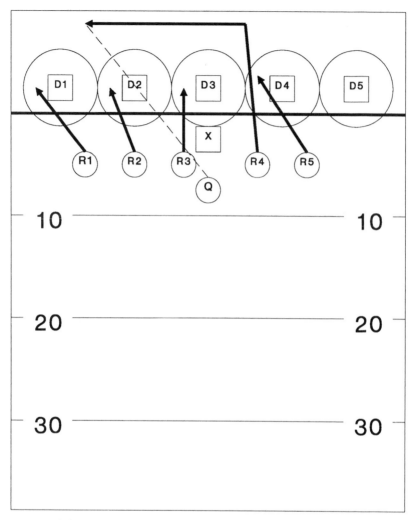

Diagram 18: Q throws over the Goal Line Zone.

7 Running Plays

To run for big yardage against a man-to-man defense, you must clear a side to run to and get the runner past his or her defender. Both are taken care of in the play shown in Diagram 19 on the next page, the **in-motion blocker run**.

By lining up three receivers on the left side and sending the fourth receiver, R4, in motion, the whole right side of the field has been opened up for Q to run. The only thing standing in the way of a long touchdown run by Q is the rusher. But the rusher is taken care of by a block from R4.

"Hey, what about D4?" you might ask. "Won't D4 stop Q?"

Probably not. That's because when R4 goes in motion, so does D4. D4's momentum takes D4 away from where Q will be running. Q should be able to get around the corner and up the field.

Another good running play is the **reverse**, shown in Diagram 20. In this play, the quarterback runs to one side of the field and then laterals back to a receiver (R4 in the diagram), who runs around to the other side of the field.

There are two keys to making this play work. First, R2 must block the runner's defender (D4 in the diagram). Second, R4 must catch the lateral deep enough behind the line of scrimmage to make sure that R4 gets around the rusher.

If you're the quarterback and you're faster than the rusher, you may want to forget about having a receiver block for you.

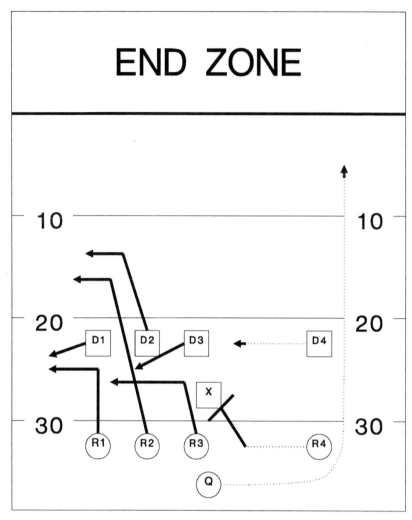

Diagram 19: On "Set," R4 starts in motion, bringing D4 to the middle of the field. On "Hike," R4 blocks X and Q runs up the right side.

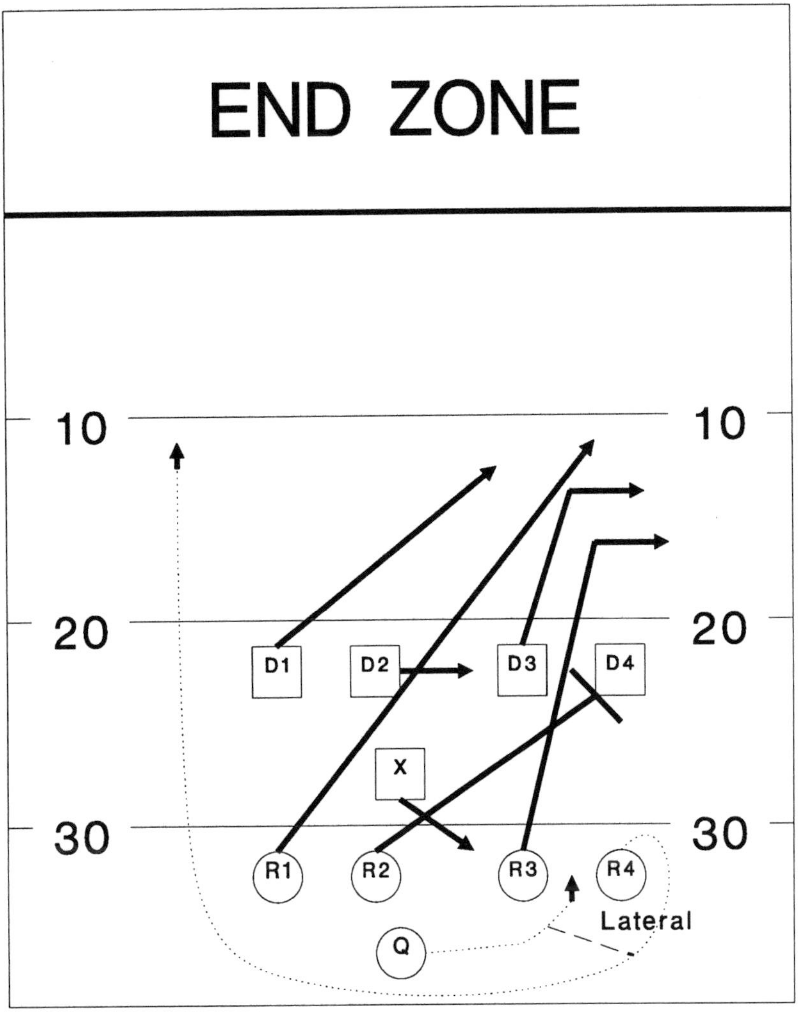

Diagram 20: The Reverse

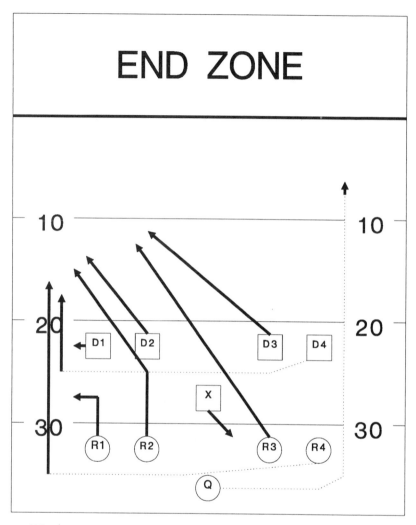

Diagram 21: Q clears the right side and then races past X for the touchdown.

In that case, just clear a side to run to by lining up your receivers on the other side of the field. This is known as the **clear right** or **clear left**, depending on which side you clear.

To hide that you are clearing a side, you may want to start out with one receiver on the side you plan to run to. Then send that receiver in motion to the other side of the field before calling "Hike." You could even start with two receivers on the side you'll be running to. Take a look at Diagram 21.

Before we leave this section on running, here's a word about running against a zone defense: *Don't*—especially if you need long yardage. Running usually doesn't work well against a zone because the defenders sit back and wait for the action. As soon as they realize you are running the ball, they will all come up and stop you for little or no gain.

8 *Razzle-Dazzle Plays*

Sometimes you can score an easy touchdown by fooling the other team with a **razzle-dazzle** play.

One of the best razzle-dazzle plays is the **hook-and-ladder**, shown in Diagram 22 on the next page. The hook-and-ladder will work best against a man-to-man defense. As you can see from the diagram, R1 runs a post and then hooks back to the quarterback.

When R1 comes back on the hook pattern, Q throws the ball. Q waits for the rusher to turn to watch where the ball was thrown, and then Q races to the outside of where R1 catches the ball. Immediately after catching the ball, R1 laterals it to Q. If all goes according to plan, Q will have clear sailing to the end zone.

Unfortunately, most offenses won't call this play until they need a miracle, like when it's fourth down and they need thirty yards for a touchdown. But that's exactly when the defense will be ready for this type of play. A better time to use the hook-and-ladder would be on first or second down, when the defense is more likely to be in man-to-man coverage.

Another good razzle-dazzle play is the **option**, shown in Diagram 23 on page 91. In the option, R1 comes in motion and takes a lateral from Q. R1 then runs to the right side as if it's a running play. Q should wait a second to make the rusher believe that Q's role in the play is over. Then, Q should race up the left side of the field.

Before crossing the line of scrimmage, R1 will have the option of running, passing to R2 on a post pattern, or passing back across the field to Q on a fly pattern.

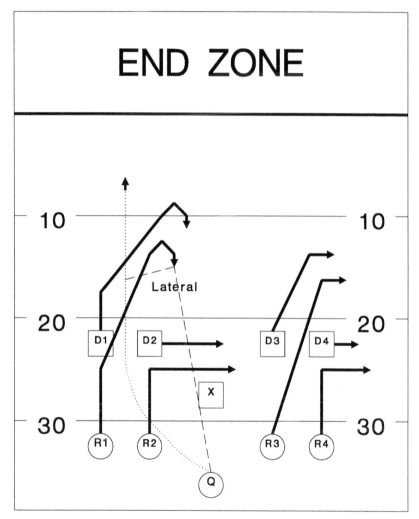

Diagram 22: The Hook-and-Ladder. Q passes the ball to R1, who then laterals the ball back to Q.

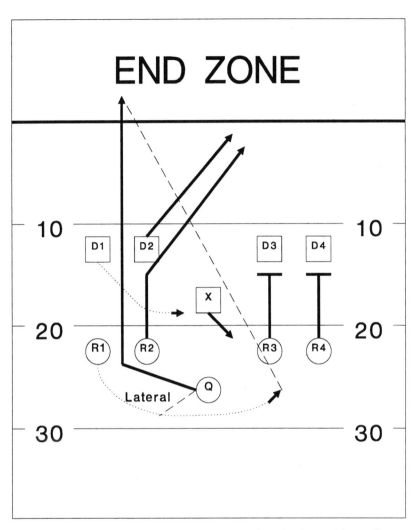

Diagram 23: The Option Play. After taking the lateral from Q, R1 can run behind R3 and R4, pass to R2, or pass back to Q.

9 *Calling Audibles*

Usually, a quarterback will call a play in the **huddle** before coming up to the line of scrimmage. In that case, all the quarterback has to do to start the play is yell "Ready-Set-Hike."

But a heads-up quarterback who spots a weakness in the defense will change the play at the line of scrimmage, by calling an **"audible."** An audible is a coded play that the quarterback yells to the receivers. It's called an audible because they can *hear* it.

For example, let's say the quarterback called a down-and-out pattern for one of the receivers. But at the line of scrimmage, the quarterback sees that the receiver's defender is playing the receiver very tightly. In that case, the quarterback may want to bark out an audible that tells the receiver to race by the defender for a long pass.

Of course, if he just yelled out "Hey, go long!," it would give the play away. That's where audibles come in.

Agreeing on the Audibles

Before coming up to the line of scrimmage, you need to agree with your teammates on the audibles you will use. Although you could make up all kinds of audibles to call just about any play you could imagine, it's best to start with something simple.

One simple system begins with assigning a different number to each receiver. To help everyone remember the numbers, you may want to number your receivers from left to right, the way they line up at the line of scrimmage.

Then, to complete the system, you will need to assign a number for each of the different long pass patterns you will want to be able to call. You can use "1" for a flag pattern, "2" for a fly, and "3" for a post. Now, your system of audibles is complete and you are ready to go up to the line of scrimmage.

Checking the Defense

At the line of scrimmage, the quarterback checks the defense to see if any defender is covering his or her receiver very closely at the line of scrimmage. If that is the case, the quarterback then decides which long pattern to call for that receiver.

In Diagram 24, for example, since defender D3 is overplaying R3 to the inside of the field, R3 would probably have a better chance of getting free to the outside. A flag pattern would be the best bet. Now the quarterback is ready to call the audible.

Calling the Audible

To call the audible that tells R3 to run a flag pattern instead of the down-and-out that was called in the huddle, the quarterback needs to yell out the receiver's number ("3" for R3) followed by the number of the pattern he wants the receiver to run ("1" for a flag pattern). So, in this case, the quarterback would yell out "3-1" or "Thirty-One."

Of course, if you use a simple system of audibles like this, it won't take long for the defenders to start figuring out what you are doing. So you'd better throw in some fake audibles to fool them.

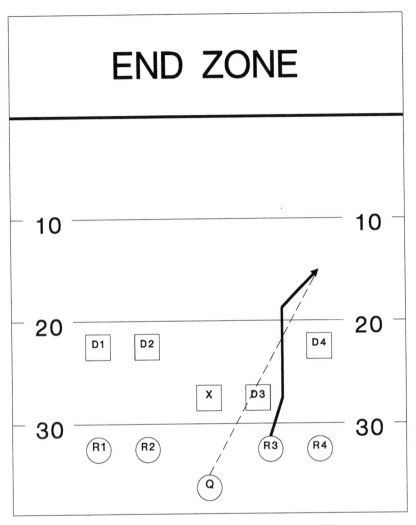

Diagram 24: Q yells out "Blue Thirty-one" to tell R3 to run a Flag pattern.

One way to do this is to add a "hot color" to your system of audibles. The hot color tells the receivers which one of a group of audibles is the "real" one.

For example, let's say that red is your hot color. If the quarterback yells "Blue 32, Green 41, Red 22," the receivers know that the "real" audible is "22" because red is the hot color. In that case, R2 will be running a fly pattern.

To make sure the defenders aren't figuring out your audibles, change the numbers of your receivers from time to time. Changing the hot color from time to time is also a good idea.

DEFENSIVE PLAYS

10 *Playing a Zone Defense*

To confuse the offense, you may want to use a zone defense from time to time. It's also a good idea to use a zone defense to stop receivers who have been getting free on criss cross patterns.

In a zone defense, each defender is responsible for a specific portion or "zone" of the field. The defenders (other than the rusher who guards the quarterback) do not cover specific receivers.

To play a zone defense, each defender goes to his or her zone and then waits. Unlike in a man-to-man defense, where each defender watches his or her receiver and not the quarterback, in a zone defense each defender keeps glancing back at the quarterback while keeping track of any receivers coming into his or her zone.

The defenders will want to try to read the quarterback's eyes to guess where the ball will be thrown. Sometimes a defender can pick up an easy interception if the quarterback "telegraphs" where he or she is throwing the ball.

During the play, each defender should talk to the defenders nearby and let them know if a receiver is coming their way.

Then, as soon as the ball is in the air, the defenders try to intercept it or knock it down, or tag the receiver if the pass is completed.

The defender tries to knock down the pass.

The best time to use a zone defense is on third or fourth down when the offense needs long yardage. The worst time to use the zone is when the offense needs to gain only a few yards. In that case, a smart receiver will beat the zone by merely finding a seam and turning back to the quarterback for a short pass.

Keep in mind that a zone defense works better with more players. That's because with more players, each defender will be responsible for a smaller zone, and there will be more defenders for the quarterback to throw between. It's pretty tough to play a zone if you have fewer than five players per team.

If you have five players per team, you can play a **2-2 zone**, as shown in Diagram 25 on page 100. As noted earlier, when describing a zone, the first number refers to the number of pass defenders playing close to the line of scrimmage and the second number refers to the deeper pass defenders. You don't assign a number to the rusher.

When you play a zone defense, you need to be prepared for a smart offensive team, which will try to overload your defense by flooding one of the defender's zones with more than one receiver. In that case, the defender whose zone is empty will need to help out by moving over to the flooded zone. Of course, the defender who is helping out must still keep an eye on his or her own zone in case a receiver runs back that way or the quarterback races around the rusher.

The zone works better with six or more players per team. If you have six players per team, you can run a **2-3 zone** (Diagram 26) or a **3-2 zone** (Diagram 27).

With seven players per team, you can use a **3-3 Zone** (Diagram 28). With eight players you can use a **4-3 zone** (Diagram 29) to really clog up the middle of the field, creating a nightmare for the quarterback.

One form of zone defense that might look like a winner until you've used it is the **goal line zone**, shown earlier in Diagram 18. In this form of zone defense, used when the offense is very close to scoring a touchdown, the defenders line up in a straight line across the goal line.

As shown in Diagram 18, however, an offense can usually beat the goal line zone easily by overloading a side and passing to the open receiver trailing across the back of the end zone.

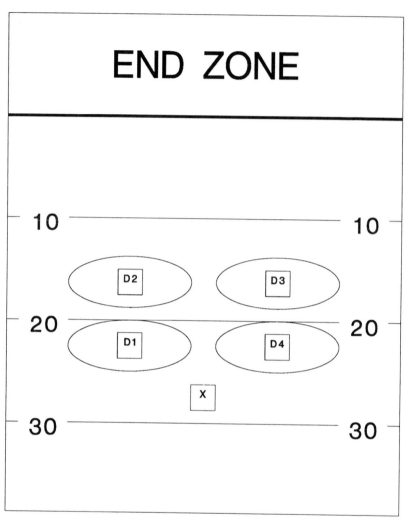

Diagram 25: The 2-2 Zone

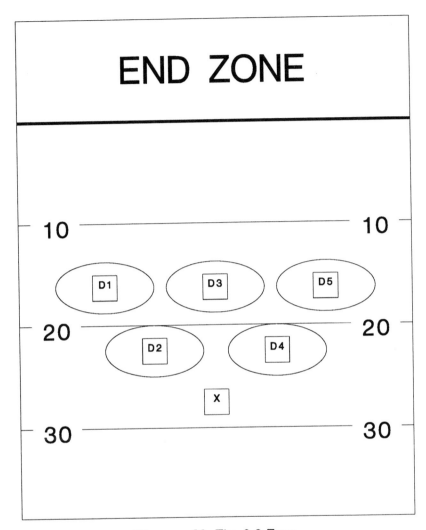

Diagram 26: The 2-3 Zone

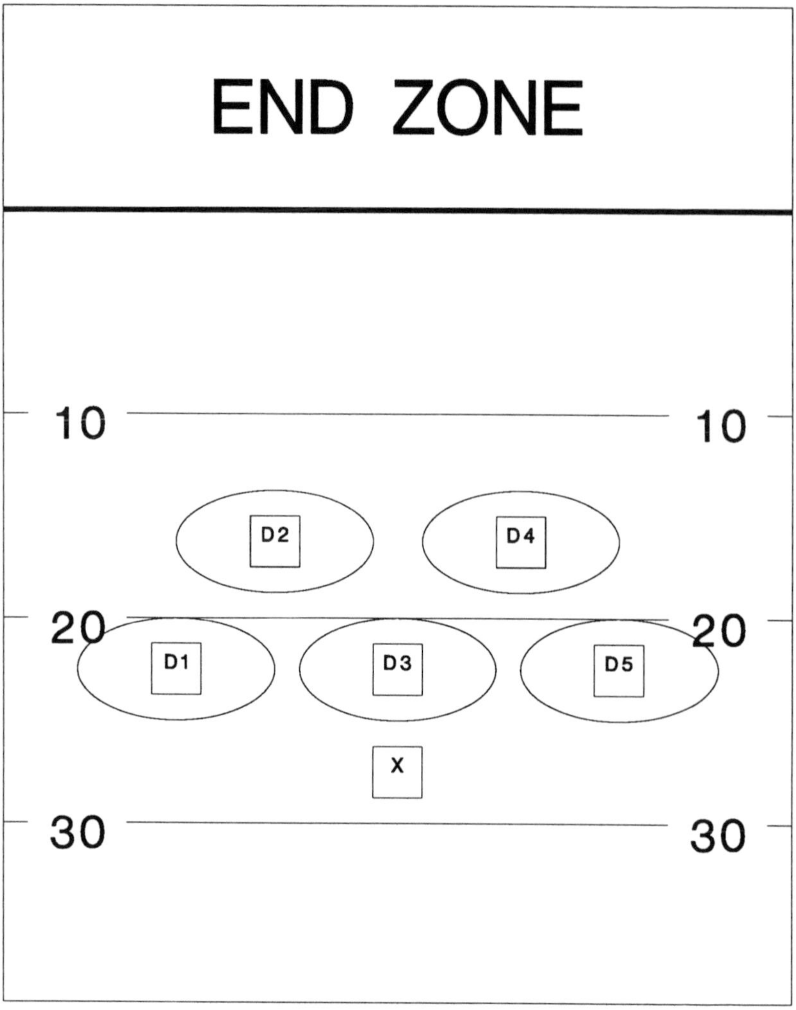

END ZONE

10 ———————————————— 10

D2   D4

20 ———————————————— 20

D1   D3   D5

X

30 ———————————————— 30

Diagram 27: The 3-2 Zone

102

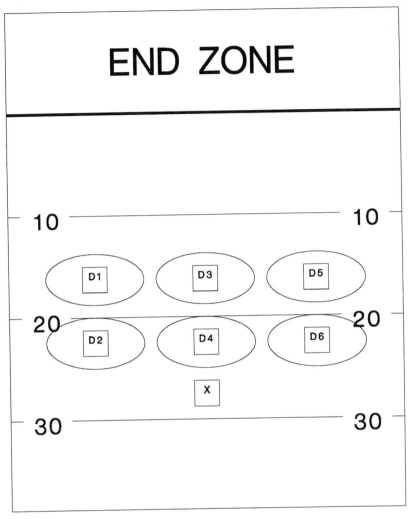

Diagram 28: The 3-3 Zone

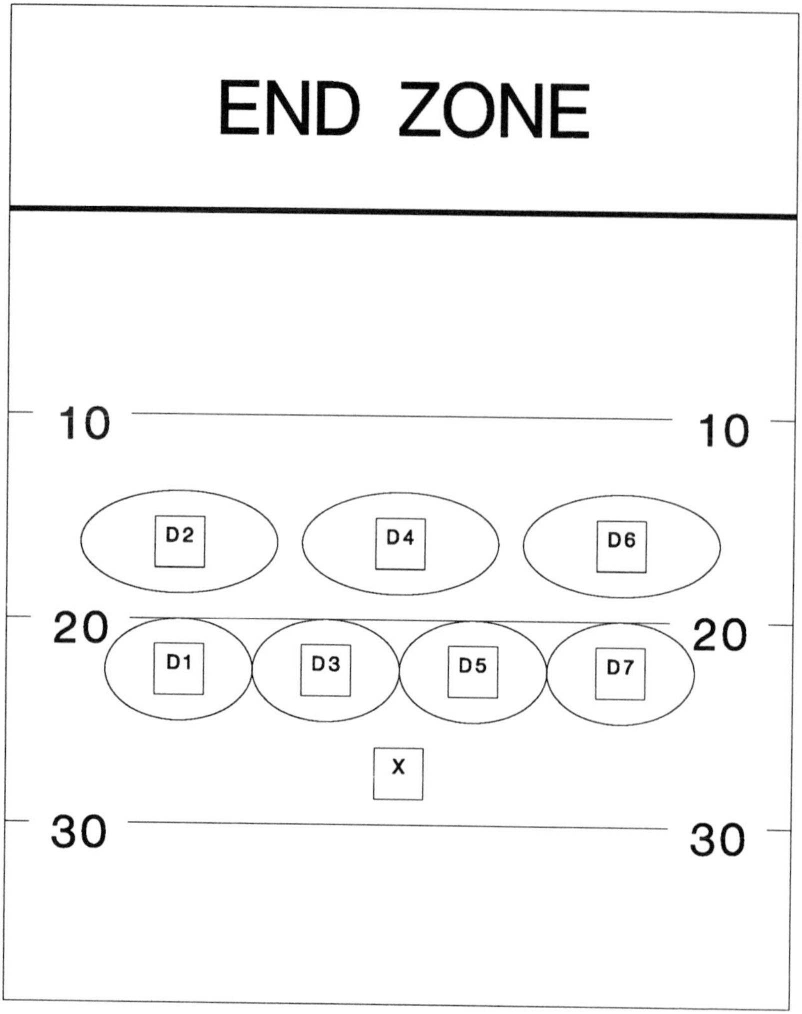

Diagram 29: The 4-3 Zone

11 *Calling the Blitz*

Most touch football games are played with the rusher counting out loud to four or five and then rushing the quarterback. A way to add excitement and strategy to your games is by allowing the defense to use the **blitz** once during each set of four downs.

A blitz is a defensive play in which a defender other than the rusher races across the line of scrimmage and tries to tag the quarterback *immediately* after the quarterback snaps the ball. In a blitz, the rusher drops back to cover the blitzing defender's receiver (if the defense is in man-to-man coverage) or zone (if the defense is in zone coverage).

To work best, a blitz should come from the quarterback's blind side—the side the quarterback has his or her back to when ready to throw. If the quarterback doesn't see the blitzing defender coming, the defender will have a great chance of sacking the quarterback for a loss of yardage. A blind-side blitz on a right-handed quarterback is shown in Diagram 30 on the next page.

Whether the defense is in man-to-man or zone coverage when the blitz is called, each of the non-blitzing defenders should cover the closest receiver very tightly as the quarterback will be forced to pass the ball quickly to avoid being sacked.

For the non-blitzing defenders, this is a great time to gamble. If the offense is caught unprepared for the blitz, a defender may be able to make an easy interception.

A blitz can be either an **outside blitz** or an **inside blitz**, depending on whether the blitzing defender comes from the outside or inside of the field (Diagrams 30 and 31).

The inside blitz often works better and is safer than the outside blitz. That's because the blitzing defender will have less ground to cover to get to the quarterback—giving the quarterback less time to throw—and because the rusher, who will be dropping back to take the blitzing defender's place, will also have less ground to cover. This cuts down on the chances of a quick pass to a wide-open receiver.

The outside blitz coming from the quarterback's blind side, however, can work very well when you think you can catch the quarterback unprepared, or when the offense needs a big chunk of yardage and will likely call a long, slow-developing pass pattern. To avoid tipping off the quarterback that the blitz is coming, try not to line up differently than you normally do.

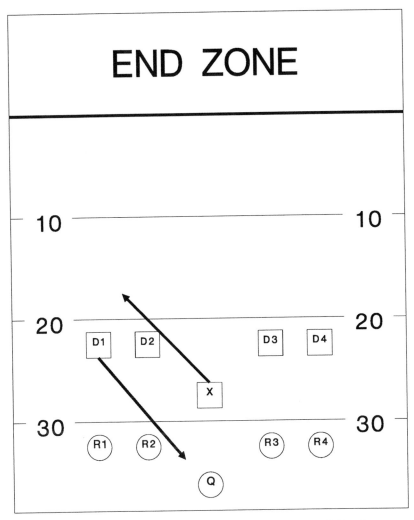

Diagram 30: D1 runs an Outside Blitz; X takes D1's place.

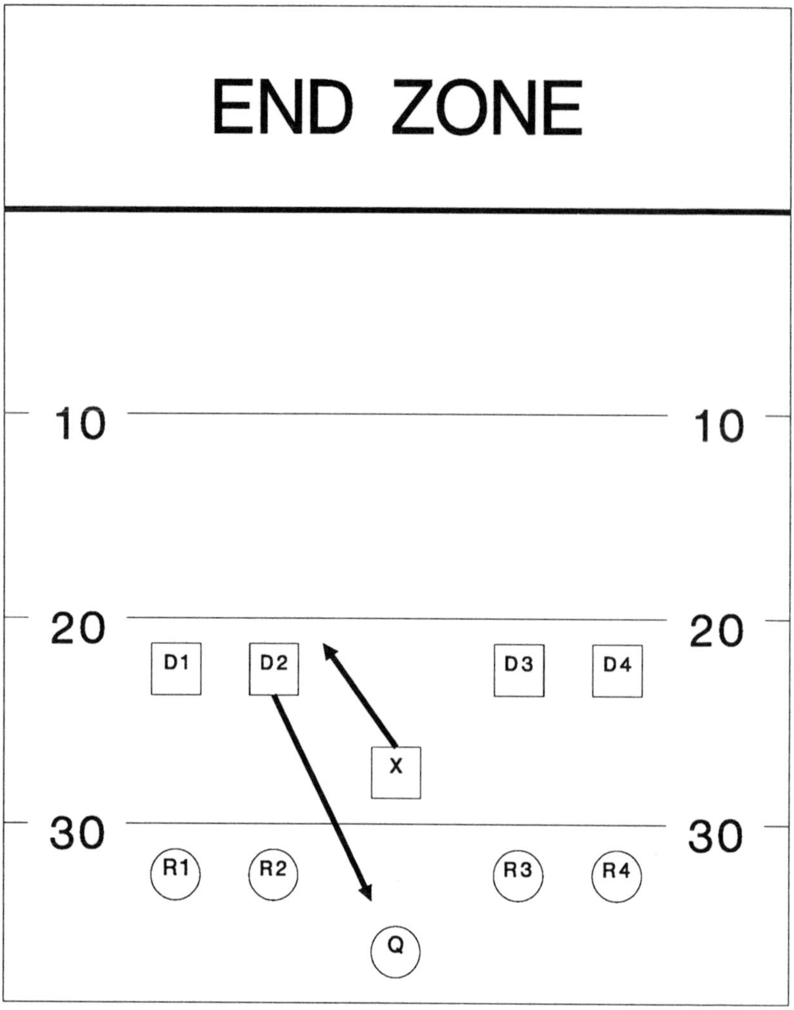

Diagram 31: D2 runs an Inside Blitz; X takes D2's place.

SAFETY TIPS

1. Try to play your games on grass fields instead of on the street or on other hard surfaces. Even in touch football, you are bound to fall from time to time.

2. Before you start playing, check the field and the area around it to make sure there isn't any broken glass, large rocks, sticks, or other things that could cause injury if someone stepped or fell on them. Also watch out for holes in the ground that someone could step into and twist an ankle or a knee. And make sure there aren't any fences or poles that someone might run into.

3. Also before you start playing, make sure you stretch so you don't pull a muscle. Some stretching exercises that I use are shown in the photographs on the next three pages. The important thing to remember about stretching is to do it slowly. Don't bounce! Otherwise, you will be pulling muscles instead of preventing muscle strains. After stretching, continue your warmup by doing some light calisthenics like jumping jacks and arm windmills.

Stretching Exercises

4. Wear all-purpose sneakers, not running shoes which are meant to go only straight ahead. Turning quickly on running shoes can sprain your ankle. On a grass field, you may want to use cleats for added traction. If you use cleats, make sure the sole of each shoe is made of one piece of molded rubber and that the cleats do not screw into the bottom of the shoe. Screw-in cleats can come loose and cause you to fall.

5. When you block a defender, block him in the chest and shoulder area—not in the head or back, or below the waist.

6. When you are playing pass defense against a receiver, make sure you know where your teammates are so you can avoid crashing into them if the receivers run a criss-cross pattern.

7. Use the rule that the play is automatically over if the ball carrier falls down or fumbles the football. It helps avoid injuries that could be caused by defenders diving on a fallen ball carrier or by players smashing into each other chasing a loose ball.

8. Don't leave your feet to tag a ball carrier or to make a block. Diving at another player is never a good idea. To avoid getting kicked in the face, don't tag a ball carrier below the waist.

9. To avoid heat exhaustion when playing in very hot weather, wear light clothing, drink plenty of cold water before, during, and after play, and take rest periods in the shade every 20-30 minutes. It's also a good idea to get your body used to the hot weather for a few days before you start playing at full speed for long periods of time.

10. After playing, you should stretch your muscles again. This will help muscles you might have strained while playing.

A SPECIAL NOTE FROM REGGIE

Although I think the plays and information in this book are super, for me, the really important thing about this book is that it's about **touch** football.

Now, don't get me wrong. I love tackle football. But I don't play tackle football unless I'm wearing all of my equipment. And neither should you. It's too easy to get hurt.

In the pros, we do everything we can to prevent injuries. We play touch football in scrimmages, and we use the finest protective equipment when we start tackling. And still we can't stop injuries from happening. I've had my share. If you need more convincing, just ask Bo. He knows.

But some injuries—the ones you'd get playing tackle football without all the proper equipment—can be prevented. It would be a real shame if your football career were cut short by this kind of injury.

I encourage you to play organized tackle football. It's a great sport. But when you're not playing in an organized league, practice your football skills by playing touch football.

GLOSSARY

AUDIBLES—coded plays that the quarterback shouts to the receivers at the line of scrimmage (for example, "Blue 32, Red 13, Hike"). See Chapter 9.

BALL CARRIER—the player with the ball.

BLITZ—a defensive play in which a defender other than the rusher races across the line of scrimmage and tries to tag the quarterback as soon as the quarterback snaps the ball.

BLOCKER—an offensive player who gets between the ball carrier and a defender to prevent the defender from tagging the ball carrier.

BUMP-AND-RUN—when a defender blocks or bumps a receiver at the line of scrimmage and then races alongside the receiver up the field.

CLIPPING—a penalty called when an offensive player blocks a defender in the back.

CRISS-CROSS—a type of pass play in which two or more receivers cross paths. Good against man-to-man coverage.

DEFENDER—a player on the defensive team.

DEFENSE—the team without the football.

DOUBLE SCREEN—when two offensive players screen the defender away from his or her receiver.

DOWN—one of a series of four plays an offense gets to score a touchdown or get a first down.

END LINE—the line at the back of each end zone.

END ZONE—the area behind each goal line.

FIRST DOWN—when an offensive team earns an additional four plays to try to score a touchdown.

FUMBLE—a dropped football.

GOAL LINE—the line in front of each team's end zone, which the other team tries to cross with the football to score a touchdown.

HUDDLE—the meeting that each team has before each play to decide what play to use.

INCOMPLETE PASS—a pass that is not caught by a receiver.

INTERCEPTION—a pass that is caught by a defender.

KICK-OFF—a ball kicked from off the ground to start the game, or after a touchdown.

LATERAL—a ball thrown sideways or backwards by a ball carrier to a teammate.

LEADING THE RECEIVER—when a quarterback throws the football in front of the receiver so the receiver doesn't have to slow up to catch the ball.

LINE OF SCRIMMAGE—the imaginary line across the field from where a play begins.

MAN-TO-MAN DEFENSE—a form of defense in which each defender covers one specific offensive player.

MIDFIELD—the imaginary line running across the middle of the field.

OFFENSE—the team with the football.

OFF-SIDES—a penalty which is called when a player from either team crosses the line of scrimmage before the quarterback snaps the ball.

ONE-HAND TOUCH FOOTBALL—a form of touch football in which a defender can tag the ball carrier with only one hand.

PASS—a football thrown forward to a teammate.

PASS INTERFERENCE—a penalty on a defender who makes contact with a receiver who is trying to catch a pass.

PICK—an illegal play in which an offensive player runs into a defender so the defender can't cover his or her receiver.

PLAY—one of a series of tries an offense gets to score a touchdown or make a first down.

PRIMARY RECEIVER—the first receiver the quarterback wants to throw the football to.

PUNT—a kick made on fourth down when the offense does not want to risk turning the ball over to the other team close to the offensive team's own end zone.

QUARTERBACK—the player who runs the offense by calling signals at the line of scrimmage, throwing passes to the receivers, and running for yardage.

READING THE QUARTERBACK'S EYES—when a defender watches where the quarterback is looking to figure out where the quarterback will throw the football.

RECEIVER—an offensive player who catches passes.

RUSHER—the defensive player who covers the quarterback.

SACK—occurs when a defender tags the quarterback behind the line of scrimmage for a loss of yardage.

SAFETY—occurs when a ball carrier is tagged behind his or her own goal line. The defense gets two points for a safety, and the ball.

SCREEN—a legal play in which an offensive player runs closely by a defender to get in his way and free up the receiver he is covering.

SECONDARY RECEIVER—a receiver the quarterback looks to throw the ball to after seeing that the primary receiver is covered.

SIDELINE—the boundary line on each side of the field.

SIGNALS—what the quarterback yells at the line of scrimmage. Signals can be nothing more than the words "Ready, Set, Hike," or they can be coded plays that the quarterback shouts to the receivers (for example, "Blue 32, Red 13, Hike"). See Chapter 9.

TACKLE FOOTBALL—a form of football that requires the defenders to force the ball carrier to the ground in order to stop a play.

TWO-HAND TOUCH FOOTBALL—a form of touch football that requires a defender to tag the ball carrier with both hands.

ZONE DEFENSE—a form of defense in which each defender is responsible for a specific zone of the field instead of a specific offensive player.

RECOMMENDED FOOTBALL READING

All About Football (Putnam).

The First Book of Football by John Madden (Crown).

Football for Young Players and Parents by Joe Namath (Simon & Schuster).

Football Rules Illustrated (Simon & Schuster).

From First Down to Touchdown: The Official NFL Beginner's Guide to Football by David Boss and Jim Natal (Gallery Books).

The Illustrated NFL Playbook (Workman Publishing).

Sports Illustrated Football: Winning Defense by Bud Wilkinson (NAL).

Sports Illustrated Football: Winning Offense by Bud Wilkinson (NAL).

The Story of Football by Dave Anderson (Morrow).

Youth League Football: Coaching and Playing by Jack Bicknell (Athletic Institute).

Youth League Passing and Receiving by Ken Anderson and Bruce Coslet (Athletic Institute).

FOOTBALL ORGANIZATIONS

If you are between the ages of 7 and 16 and would like some information about playing organized tackle football or flag football (a form of football where you have to grab the ball carrier's flag from off his belt to stop the play), contact Pop Warner Football, 1315 Walnut Street, Suite 1632, Philadelphia, Pennsylvania 19107; (215) 735-1450.

If you are an adult and would like some information about playing organized touch football or flag football, contact the following organizations:

National Touch Football Leagues
1039 Coffey Court
Crestwood, Missouri 63126
(314) 621-0777

United States Flag Football League
5834 Pine Tree Drive
Sanibel, Florida 33957
(813) 472-0544

ABOUT THE AUTHORS

Larry Reid

Larry Reid is a full-time attorney in the Washington, D.C. area who has written a video script and various articles. He obtained his undergraduate degree from Duke University and his law degree from George Washington University, where he was a member of *The George Washington University Law Review*. Larry has been playing football, including intramural flag football and organized tackle football, since he was in grade school and continues to play touch football every Saturday morning during the football season with other weekend warriors.

Reggie White

Reggie White, of the Philadelphia Eagles, is the premier defensive lineman in the National Football League. An All-Pro for the past five straight years, he holds the NFC single season sack record (21) and was voted NFL Player of the Year in 1988. While at the University of Tennessee, Reggie achieved All-American status and was named Southeastern Conference Player of the Year.

Known as the "Minister of Defense" because he is a licensed Baptist Minister, Reggie is also a well respected community leader. Recently, he and his wife, Sara, founded a home for unwed mothers. Reggie is also involved with the Eagles Fly for Leukemia Campaign and does public service announcements warning about drugs and alcohol. In *The Reggie White Touch Football Playbook,* he combines his football expertise with his caring for players of all ages.

About the Illustrator and Photographer

Millicent Tuman, who provided the illustrations for this book, studied art at Brooklyn College, Brooklyn Museum, and Pratt Institute. She has done the illustrations for other works and has a diverse list of art credits, including teaching pastels and oils, hand painting on fabric, and jewelry design.

Barbara Kinney, who provided the photographs for this book, is a free-lance photographer based in Washington, D.C. Prior to taking off on her own, she worked as picture editor/ photographer with *USA Today*, where she covered various sporting events, including the Super Bowl, the U.S. Open, the NCAA Basketball Regionals, and the Boston Marathon. She currently specializes in editorial, corporate, and advertising photography.

Give a gift of safety and fun to the football players in your life

ORDER FORM

YES, I want to share this terrific new book, *The Reggie White Touch Football Playbook*. Please send me _____ copies at $9.95, plus $2.50 shipping and handling. Virginia residents please add 45 cents sales tax. Allow three weeks for delivery.

Name _____

Phone _____

Organization _____

Address _____

City/State/Zip _____

Send your check or MO: Warrenton Press, Inc.
31 Pepper Tree Court
Warrenton, VA 22186

For information on bulk quantity discounts
or special handling, please call
(703) 347-2856

Call credit card order to 1-800-444-2524, Ext. 10